TAOISM, CONFUCIANISM AND BUDDHISM

China Ancient History 3rd Grade Children's Ancient History

BABY PROFESSOR

EDUCATION KIDS

Speedy Publishing LLC

40 E. Main St. #1156

Newark, DE 19711

www.speedypublishing.com

Copyright 2017

TAOISM, CONFUCIANISM, AND BUDDHISM are the three major philosophies or religions that have shaped most of the history and ideas of Ancient China. In this book, we will be learning about each of the three philosophies.

TAOISM

WHAT IS THE DEFINITION OF TAO?

Pronounced dow, Tao means "way".

The Taoists believe that the Way is the underlying spiritual force of the universe and considered to be a part of all things. While it is believed to be a part of all things, it is considered to be larger than all things and is believed to be the ultimate reality.

YIN AND YANG, SYMBOL OF TAOISM

LAO TZE

HOW DID TAOISM START?

Lao Tze, who was a Chinese philosopher and the Supreme master started this religion during the 6th century BCE. He lived during the same time period as Confucius, who was another Chinese philosopher.

It is believed that Lao Tze decided one day to leave his job and left on an ox towards the west. The guardian of a mountain pass asked to write about his teachings and the result was the Doodejing, which is the sacred book of Tao. In addition, this is why you will find figures and statues of Lao Tze riding an ox.

YUANXUAN TAOIST TEMPLE, CHINA

Taoism is practiced today by approximately 5 million people located in Japan, China, Hong Kong, Taiwan, Vietnam, and Malaysia. It is common for Taoism to be linked with Buddhism and Confucianism.

WHAT ARE THEIR BELIEFS?

People that practice Taoism believe they should live in harmony with the Way or Tao. If they believe in this philosophy they will unite with the Tao, their soul will be free, and they will become an Immortal.

COUPLE PRAYING

Taoists originally believed that there was only the Tao, and no gods or goddesses. Over time, however, they started to worship Lao Tze and other great Taoist teachers. They started to worship the forces of nature, including the tides, stars, moon, and sun.

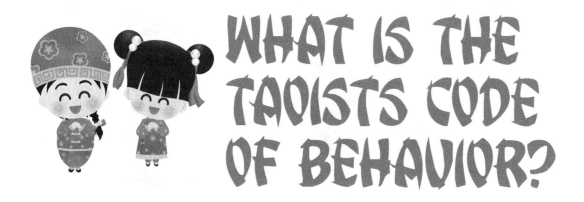

WHAT IS THE TAOISTS CODE OF BEHAVIOR?

It is believed by Taoists that good actions will result in a better life for their soul, and they follow guides and rules for the way they live. It is not permissible for them to steal, tell lies, drink alcohol, commit murder, or commit adultery.

In addition, they have a good deeds list to guide them further in the way they live their lives. It is encouraged that they love their parents, obey their elders, help others act, be tolerant, maintain excellent mental and physical shape, act without thinking of themselves, maintain body and mind self-control, and help others act. In other words, they should act selflessly.

HOW DOES T'AI CHI CH'UAN RELATE TO TAOISM?

T'ai Chi is a series of slow-moving, controlled exercises that discipline the mind and the body and is both a form of meditation as well as a form of physical exercise, that was created by a Taoist. It is practiced by millions today, particularly Chinese.

MIDDLE-AGED CHINESE MEN PRACTICE T'AI CHI IN CHINA

WHAT IS THE MEANING OF THE YIN/YANG TAO SYMBOL?

The Yin/Yang Tao symbol stands for the harmonious interaction of the yin (male) and the yang (female) opposing forces of the Universe.

CONFUCIUS

Not much is known about the early life of Confucius. Born in 551 BC in the state of Lu to a soldier named Kong, who died when Confucius was only three. Confucius spent his remaining childhood raised by his mother, living in poverty.

STATUE OF CONFUCIUS

His family was a part of the "shi" which was an expanding middle class of people, considered to be above the common peasants, but not a part of the nobility. This provided Confucius with a different outlook on life than most others. He believed people should be rewarded and promoted based on their talents, not the family to which they were born.

HIS EARLY CAREER

Confucius did not begin as a wise teacher, but had previously worked several normal jobs, including being a clerk and being a shepherd. He eventually went to work for a government entity. He started this career as a small-town governor and moved up the ladder becoming a top-level advisor for the government.

THE CONFUCIUS TEMPLE AREA IN NANJING, CHINA

HOW DID CONFUCIANISM BEGIN?

K'ung Fu-tzu, was a Chinese philosopher, also known as Confucius (the Western version), who believed that if the people that lived in society exhibited "beautiful conduct", it would become a perfect society.

Born 551 B.C.E., Confucius held a job with the government that he chose to leave so that he was able to devote his entire life instructing people how to behave. More than 5 million people, mostly in the Far East and China, now practice Confucianism.

TAIPEI CONFUCIUS TEMPLE IN DALONGDONG, TAIPEI, TAIWAN

GRANDDAUGHTER KISSING HER OLD GRANDMOTHER

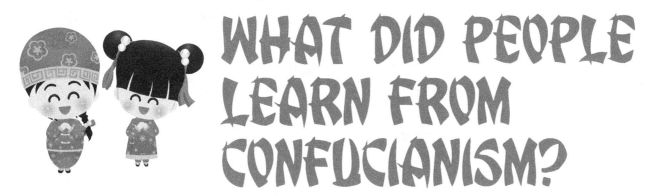

WHAT DID PEOPLE LEARN FROM CONFUCIANISM?

People were taught five basic behaviors from Confucius:

- Be considerate to others at all times.
- Show respect for your ancestors.

- Achieve for balance and harmony in all things.
- Avoid extreme emotions and behaviors.
- You will be in touch with spiritual forces throughout the universe, which includes nature, if you live with harmony and peace.

YOUNG MAN HELPING A SENIOR GENTLEMAN WITH HIS GROCERIES

Listed below are the five basic virtues taught by Confucius:

1) kindness
2) righteousness
3) sobriety
4) wisdom
5) trustworthiness

In addition, Confucius taught that the well-being of others plays a major role in your own well-being. This idea is known as Jen and it stresses the importance of showing loyalty and courtesy to others.

Confucius also teaches that one's family and their family values are quite important. Children are instructed to be respectful to their parents as well as obeying their parents.

GIRL HELPING HER MOM DO THE HOUSE CHORES

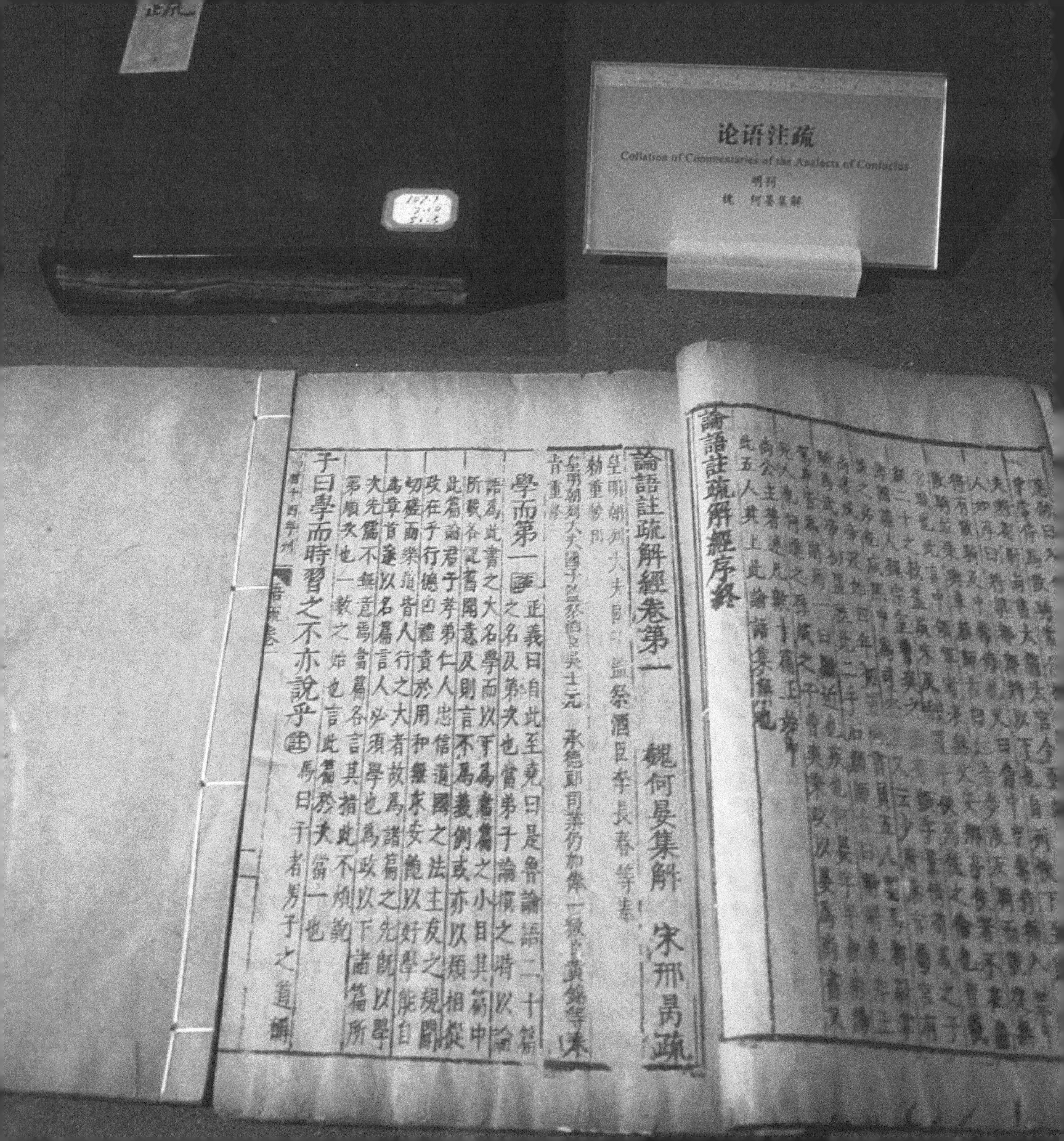

論語註疏解經序終

論語註疏解經卷第一

學而第一

魏何晏集解

宋邢昺疏

子曰學而時習之不亦說乎

CONFUCIAN SCRIPTURES

Confucian scriptures are contained in five different texts that include history, poems, sayings, and rituals.

WHERE DO THE CONFUCIANS WORSHIP?

Some believe that Confucianism consists more of being a moral person than it is a practice of spirituality. Following Confucius's death, however, temples were built to honor him and they have ceremonies in the temples. It was believed by Confucius that "Heaven is the author of the virtue that is in me".

MEMORIAL ARCH IN NANJING CONFUCIUS TEMPLE,CHINA.

He believed this to mean that heaven is a form of god, the supreme being, or the god who instilled virtue in each of us. This also helps to show how this philosophy is more than simply a form of behavior. In addition, aspects of Taoism and Buddhism, over time, have had an influence over Confucianism. There are many people that practice the blend of these three religions.

Listed here are only a few of Confucius's many popular sayings that are still famous today:

- Forget injuries, never forget kindnesses.
- It does not matter how slowly you go so long as you do not stop.
- Our greatest glory is not in never falling, but in getting up every time we do.
- When anger rises, think of the consequences.
- Everything has its beauty but not everyone sees it.

BUDDHISM

Buddhism started 2,500 years ago in India and is still the leading world religion of the East. There are more than 360 million followers worldwide and today there are more than a million American Buddhists. In addition, the concepts of Buddhism have had influence over western culture, particularly in the areas of nonviolence and mediation.

The practice of Buddhism is based on Siddharta Gautama's teachings, who was a Nepali prince living around 500 BCE. In accordance with Buddhist tradition, this young, sheltered prince became shocked when observing life outside of the palace walls, and he left this luxurious life to find answers. He eventually succeeded, and became the Buddha – also referred to as the "Enlightened One". He went on to spend his remaining life of 45 years teaching about the dharma (the path from suffering to liberation) and established the sangha (which was a community of monks).

BUDDHA GAUTAMA

Throughout its extensive history, Buddhism has been seen in several different forms. Some of these forms emphasize the worship of deities and rituals, and other reject completely the gods and rituals in favor pure meditation. However, all Buddhism forms share the same respect for the Buddha teachings as well as the goal of achieving the end of suffering and the cycle of rebirth.

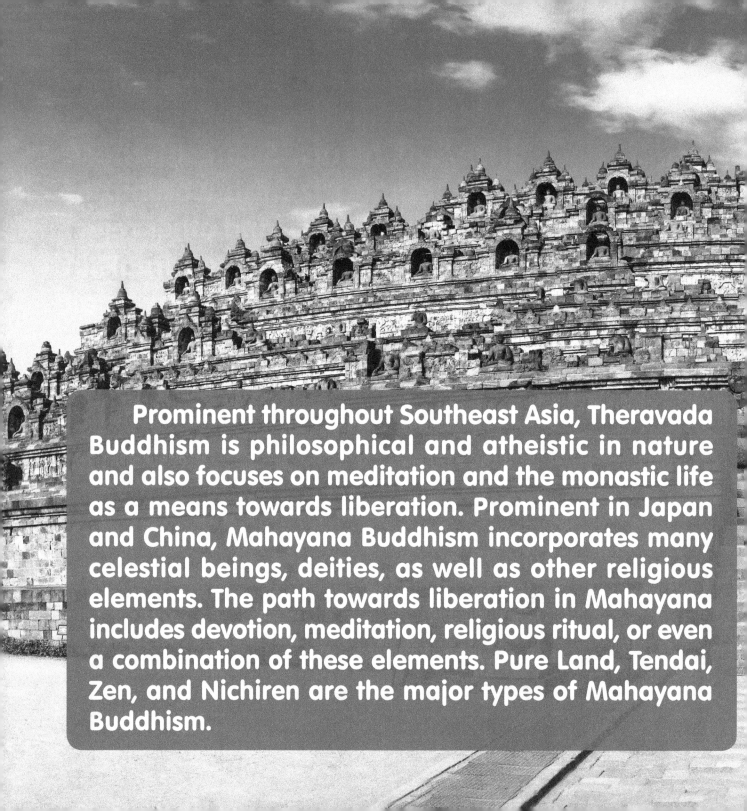

Prominent throughout Southeast Asia, Theravada Buddhism is philosophical and atheistic in nature and also focuses on meditation and the monastic life as a means towards liberation. Prominent in Japan and China, Mahayana Buddhism incorporates many celestial beings, deities, as well as other religious elements. The path towards liberation in Mahayana includes devotion, meditation, religious ritual, or even a combination of these elements. Pure Land, Tendai, Zen, and Nichiren are the major types of Mahayana Buddhism.

MAHAYANA BUDDHIST TEMPLE IN MAGELANG, INDONESIA

KARMA

Additionally, Buddhists believe in Karma, which concepts indicates that every action has a consequence. This means that your actions taken today will return to you in the future to either help you or hurt you, dependent upon whether the actions you took today were good or bad.

While these three religions are somewhat similar in their beliefs and teachings, they are quite different in their own ways. For additional information about these three philosophies, you can visit your local library, research the internet, and ask questions of your teachers, family, and friends.

CPSIA information can be obtained
at www.ICGtesting.com
Printed in the USA
BVHW060042220722
642529BV00008B/223

9 781541 916050